World Wildlife Alphabet

Alfabeto de la Fauna Mundial

MARTHA J. WEIL

ISBN 978-1-962363-61-7 (Paperback)
ISBN 978-1-962363-62-4 (Ebook)

Inquiries and Book Orders should be addressed to:

Leavitt Peak Press
17901 Pioneer Blvd Ste L #298, Artesia, California 90701
Phone #: 2092191548

A a

arctic wolf

lobo ártico

B b

buffalo

búfalo

2

C c

cockatoo

cacatúa

D d

dolphin

delfín

E e

elephant

elefante

F f

fruit bat

murciélago frugívoro

Gg

gorilla

gorila

Hh

horse

caballo

I i

impala

impala

J j

jaguar

jaguar

K k

koala bear

koala

L l

lemur

lémur

12

Mm

monarch butterfly

mariposa monarca

N n

newt

tritón

Oo

orca

orca

P p

panda bear

panda

Qq

quetzal

quetzal

R r

rabbit

conejo

S s

snake

serpiente

T t

tiger

tigre

U u

urchin

erizo de mar

V v

vulture

buitre

Ww

wombat

wómbat

X x

xantis yak

yak xantis

24

Y y

yellow-bellied sapsucker

chupasavia oscuro

Z z

zebra

zebra